Recycle

Kay Barnham

Crabtree Publishing Company
www.crabtreebooks.com

Crabtree Publishing Company

www.crabtreebooks.com

Editors: Penny Worms, Molly Aloian, Michael Hodge
Senior Design Manager: Rosamund Saunders
Designer: Ben Ruocco, Tall Tree Ltd

Photo Credits:
Alamy: p. 16 (Daphne Christelis), p. 17 (Tina Manley), p. 21 (Neil Setchfield), p. 25 (Simon de Trey-White), p. 29 (Jim West). Corbis images: p. 6 (Chris Lisle), p. 20 (Alain Nogues). Digital Vision: p. 14. Ecoscene: p. 7 (Wayne Lawler), p. 10 (John Wilkinson), p. 12 (John Wilkinson), p. 13 (Sally Morgan), p. 19 (Angela Hampton), p. 23 (Sally Morgan), p. 24 (Nick Hawkes), p. 27 (Kevin King), p. 28 (Rosemary Greenwood). Getty images: p. 15 (Michael Paul), p. 18 (Dennis O'Clair), p. 26 (Alistair Berg). istockphoto.com: cover, p. 14. Rex Features: p. 9, (Roy Garner), p. 11 (Action Press). Wayland Picture Library: title page and p. 4, p. 5, p. 8, p. 22.

Library and Archives Canada Cataloguing in Publication

Barnham, Kay
  Recycle / Kay Barnham.

(Environment action)
Includes index.
ISBN 978-0-7787-3659-2 (bound).--ISBN 978-0-7787-3669-1 (pbk.)

  1. Recycling (Waste, etc.)--Juvenile literature. 2. Refuse and refuse disposal--Juvenile literature. I. Title. II. Series: Barnham, Kay. Environment action.

TD794.5.B37 2007   j363.72'82   C2007-904689-4

Library of Congress Cataloging-in-Publication Data

Barnham, Kay.
  Recycle / Kay Barnham.
    p. cm. -- (Environment action)
  Includes index.
  ISBN-13: 978-0-7787-3659-2 (rlb)
  ISBN-10: 0-7787-3659-8 (rlb)
  ISBN-13: 978-0-7787-3669-1 (pbk)
  ISBN-10: 0-7787-3669-5 (pbk)
  1. Recycling (Waste, etc.)--Juvenile literature. I. Title. II. Series.

TD794.5.B365 2008
363.72'82--dc22

                                2007030000

Crabtree Publishing Company

www.crabtreebooks.com   1-800-387-7650

Published in Canada
Crabtree Publishing
616 Welland Ave.
St. Catharines, Ontario
L2M 5V6

Published in the United States
Crabtree Publishing
PMB16A
350 Fifth Ave., Suite 3308
New York, NY, 10118

Published by CRABTREE PUBLISHING COMPANY
Copyright © **2008**

Contents

What is recycling?

Recycling is using something again instead of throwing it away. When old bottles and jars are recycled, they are **melted down** and made into new bottles and jars.

△ Many of the things that we throw away could be recycled.

Recycling is something that everyone can do. You can recycle at home, at school, and at work. Stop and think before you put things in the garbage! Look at them carefully. Could they be recycled?

△ A lot of things, including cans, plastic bottles, cardboard, vegetable peels, and batteries, can be recycled.

Why recycle?

There are a lot of reasons to recycle. It is often cheaper to recycle than it is to make new things. Recycling is also a very good way of helping the **environment**. It saves natural materials, such as trees, oil, and water.

△ Encourage your parents to buy secondhand furniture. Doing so will help save trees.

We get wood from trees to make paper, furniture, and buildings. Wood can be burned as **fuel**. Chopping down trees destroys animals' homes and damages natural areas. It can even affect the weather and cause **floods**.

△ People have destroyed or cut down almost three quarters of Indonesia's **rainforests**.

FACT!

Metal, glass, and plastic are all made from **natural materials**.

Dealing with garbage

A lot of our garbage is taken away and put into **landfills**. Landfills are large holes dug into the ground. When a landfill is full, a layer of dirt is spread over the top. It can take hundreds of years—and sometimes much longer—for the garbage to break down and disappear. Some garbage never disappears.

△ Garbage trucks collect garbage from outside our homes and businesses.

People often throw away paper, plastic, wood, metal, food, glass, and **waste** from gardens. All of these things could be recycled, however. As landfills become full, we may run out of places to put our garbage.

If people recycle things, we will not need so much space for garbage.

FACT!

It is thought that disposable diapers take 500 years to break down. Cloth diapers can be reused.

A cleaner world

Pollution is dirty and unhealthy air, land, or water. People cause pollution when they burn, bury, or flush away waste. Burning garbage in **incinerators** turns it into **ash**, which is smaller and easier to manage. These fires ~~can~~ send *from factories* harmful gases into the air, however.

△ Some experts think that air pollution is causing **global warming**. Global warming is making the Earth too hot.

△ Polluting rivers and streams harms plants and animals.

When you flush the toilet or pull out a plug after a bath, the water flows to a **wastewater treatment works**. The water is cleaned so that it can be used again. Unfortunately, dirty water from **factories** often pours straight into rivers, streams, and oceans.

Recycling paper

Paper is made from wood **pulp**. Millions of valuable trees have been cut down to make paper. In some parts of the world, trees are still being destroyed. People now use specially planted trees to make most new paper. No new trees are used to make recycled paper!

△ You can use both sides of the paper or buy recycled paper for your letters and drawings.

Letters, newspapers, magazines, cardboard, and **junk mail** are just some of the types of paper that can be recycled over and over again. Paper is mixed with water and mashed to pulp. It is cleaned. The pulp is then rolled thinly to make new paper.

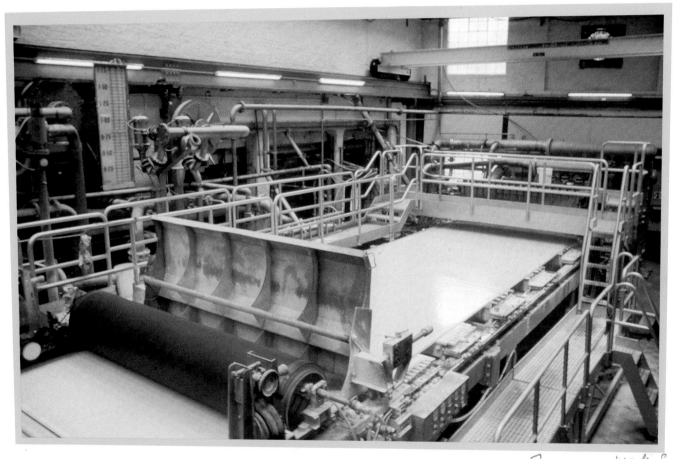

This paper mill is making recycled paper.

Recycling glass

Every day, people throw away millions of glass bottles and jars. This glass can all be recycled. Glass is perfect for recycling. No matter how many times it is melted and reshaped, it will never become weak.

 In the United States, about 28 billion glass bottles and jars are thrown away every year.

△ Old glass jars can be reused. Some people fill them with tasty homemade jam.

When glass is recycled, the **temperature** of the **furnace** is cooler than it is for making new glass. Cooler temperatures save energy and reduce pollution. Fewer natural materials, such as sand and limestone, need to be used.

Recycling cans

Food and drink cans are made from steel and aluminum. Both of these metals are easy and cheap to recycle. It takes a lot of energy to **mine** aluminum and then make it into cans, foil, trays, lids, and chocolate wrappers. Recycling aluminum uses much less energy than making new aluminum does.

△ Only ten to twelve percent of the cans we use are recycled. It is important to recycle as many cans as you can.

There is a wide variety of canned food at grocery stores. All of these cans could be recycled.

Next time you visit the grocery store, look at the shelves of jars and cans— every single one will be made of some recycled material.

Recycling plastic

Plastic causes a lot of problems for the environment. Many types of plastic will never break down. Burning plastic produces poisonous smoke. Plastic is made from oil. Oil supplies will not last for ever.

Recycled plastic can be made into many things, including clothing! It takes 25 large plastic bottles to make one warm sweater.

Recycling plastic is expensive. The best thing to do with plastic is to use it again. Do not throw it away! Plastic bags can be used again and again. Your parents can buy a strong reusable shopping bag at most grocery stores.

Take a sturdy bag with you when you go shopping. It lasts much longer and is stronger too!

FACT!

Recycled plastic can be made into many things, including sleeping bags, pipes, furniture, and fences!

Recycling textiles

Textiles are clothes, sheets and pillowcases, curtains, carpets, and shoes. People often throw these items away before they are worn out. It is better to reuse or recycle textiles. Perhaps someone else could use your old textiles. Textiles can also be recycled to make clothes, furniture padding, paper, and mattresses.

△ Many charities clean and send secondhand clothes to people who need them.

△ Top fashion designers look for ideas in secondhand clothing stores. They are recycling designs!

There are stores that sell secondhand clothes to make money for different charities. Secondhand clothes are much cheaper than new clothes are. You might be able to buy a whole outfit for the price of a new pair of socks!

Reduce, reuse, recycle!

If we **reduce**, reuse, or recycle our waste, we can cut down the amount of garbage that is buried in landfills or burned in incinerators. When we reduce the amount of things we use, there is less garbage to throw away. For example, when people send letters, they use pens, paper, and envelopes. **E-mails** require no materials at all!

◁ Get creative! Reuse yogurt containers, pieces of cardboard, and egg cartons to make a sculpture.

△ If you check the labels, you can find many items made from recycled materials.

Instead of throwing old things away, we can reuse or recycle them. People can also buy items made from recycled materials, such as recycled paper, plastic wrap, and garbage bags.

Recycling at home

In a lot of towns and cities, garbage is **collected** from homes. Materials for recycling are also collected. People fill large plastic boxes and bags with newspaper, cardboard, bottles, cans, and plastic. They put these out for collection.

 Packaged foods have a lot of packaging, but loose vegetables have none at all! Plenty of packaging material could be saved if we did not buy packaged food.

Think before you throw away wrapping paper, cards, and cardboard after birthdays or Christmas. You could recycle the items or use them again. Christmas trees with roots can be planted in the garden and then used the next year.

 Old Christmas trees can be chopped up into pieces. Gardeners can spread the pieces onto soil to help plants grow.

Recycling at school

You might already recycle paper at school, but did you know that there are many other ways to help reduce waste? You can raise money for your school or a local charity simply by recycling! Some businesses will pay for aluminum cans and foil. The more you collect, the more money you will raise!

◁ Instead of drinking from a plastic bottle of water and then throwing the bottle away, refill it and use the bottle again.

Apple cores and other scraps of food will break down and make **compost**. After some time, the compost can be spread around flowers and bushes. It feeds the plants and makes them grow.

◁ Food scraps can be mixed with leaves to make a good compost.

More ideas!

Instead of throwing away old toys and **trinkets**, have a garage sale or take them to a rummage sale. To you, your belongings might be old and boring. To someone else, they will be new and exciting!

△ Selling secondhand items at rummage sales helps the environment and also raises money for charity.

△ Some charities collect old cellular telephones, fix them, and sell them again.

Charities will take more than just old clothes and books. Did you know that some charities recycle old cellular telephones, computers, stamps, and empty **printer cartridges**? Donating these items means that you can help charities raise money and recyce at the same time!

Glossary

ash The grey powder left when something is burned

collected When things are gathered together

compost Rotted vegetables and other waste that is added to soil as food for plants

e-mail A message sent from one computer to another

energy The power needed to make things work

environment The world around us

factories Buildings where people make things with machines

floods A lot of water covering land that is usually dry

fuel Things that are burned to make energy

furnace A very hot oven where things are melted

global warming The gradual increase in Earth's temperature

incinerator A very hot oven where waste is burned

junk mail Mail sent by companies to advertise their goods or services

landfills Large holes dug into the ground where waste is buried

melted down When something is changed from a solid into a liquid

mine To dig coal, metal, or other natural materials out of the ground

natural materials Things found on or in the Earth that are not made by people

pollution Dirty or unhealthy air, land, or water

printer cartridge An ink container that fits inside a printer

pulp A wet, mushy mixture

rainforest A large forest in a hot part of the world

recycling When something is not thrown away after use but is used again

reduce To make something smaller or less

reuse To use something again

temperature How hot or cold something is

textiles Anything made of fabric

trinket A piece of jewelry or an ornament

waste Something that is not needed any more

wastewater treatment works A place where waste water is cleaned

Index

Printed in the USA